Walking Through Memories

Cover design by Hopp Creative, LLC
Cover photograph by Brande N. Martin, MA

ISBN: 978-1-7360993-7-7

Table of Contents

Biography

Charlyne Blatcher Martin, MA, is a playwright, poet, freelance writer, creator and host of Comcast talk show, *"Something To Talk About."* Her plays include: *Epiphany* (finalist 2014 Rockford New Play Festival); *Crossing Bridges* (2002-World Premier at Rock Valley Studio Theatre) and recipient of 2002 Race Unity Award from the Bahai Institute Oneness of Humanity); Black History Series: *Queen Bess and Pancho Barnes* (2009-CAPA Auburn High School and Rockford Public Library); *Bravery and Courage: the Buffalo Soldiers* (2001-Midway Village Museum Center & Ethnic Heritage Museum); *Harriet Tubman: The Black Moses and the Road to Freedom* (2003-Ethnic Heritage Museum); *The Slaves* (2008-CAPA Auburn High School at Rockford College); and *A Week in August* (1997-Top 100 Stage Plays Writer's

Digest Writing Competition, 1998-New Voices in the Heartland Series-New America Theater, and 1998 Rockford College Dramatic Reading) 2005 short screenplay *"The House at 1214"* and 2003-full length screenplay, *"Right of Way"*. She worked as assistant to the playwright-in-residence and as the dramaturge at New American Theatre in Illinois, 1988-1990. Blatcher Martin was the Festival Director for the Rockford New Play Festival, The Westside Showroom, Rockford, IL 2017-2019.

Blatcher Martin has taught *"Write On Poetry"* and Shakespeare appreciation classes at the Rock Valley Community College Center for Learning in Retirement. Also, she has written poems-on-request for special occasions including weddings, anniversaries, retirements, baby blessings, and funerals.

She has written numerous articles for publications such as: Medscape; Northwest Quarterly; *Rock River Valley Insider*; *Rockford*

Register Star; *Business Profile Magazine*; *Rockford Woman*; *Sales and Marketing Strategies & News*; *Bridges Transitions*; *Foundation Magazine*; *Rock River Times; The Black Convention Magazine*; *NAT News*; *Vital Force*; and *Rockford Journal*.

Her talk show, "*Something To Talk About*", airs on Comcast. For over 20 years, she has interviewed a wide variety of guests on subjects that include: health/wellness, politics, art, education, music, cosmetology, literature, government, political science, and law enforcement.

Blatcher Martin has a Bachelor's degree in English/Literature from Rockford College (now Rockford University), Rockford, IL, and a Master's degree in Communication Studies from Northern Illinois University, De Kalb, IL. She also has various certificates and training in other fields of interest, such as aviation, conflict resolution/facilitation, dramaturgy, cooking and studying Spanish.

From The Author

Thanks to God and to Brande, my daughter, who believed that I could gather these poems in one place and have a book. I did with her help and the work of Hopp Creative.

Poems are like beautiful snapshots of things experienced. This collection contains some occasions that called for a few "words." Some of the poems and writings are for various events in my life and in the lives of others. Poetry offers itself freely to just let what's inside of you soar and burst out all over its glorious self.

Writing poetry represents times when I can just say what I feel…unbridled and seeking only to express, not to impress. So, come and take a walk with me through some of my memories. Linger awhile or skip through the pages.

No rush, no hurry. But, most of all, I hope you
enjoy the walk.

Love, Charlyne

August 10, 2020

The Invitation

You opened your door and I walked in.

I had no idea where to begin.

You invited me to sit.

You invited me to stay.

Now, I know my life began that day.

What a surprise as you helped me to see

The person who lives inside of me.

You gently coaxed me out of a shell.

You showed me a glimpse of heaven

In the place where I dwell.

I know that I am growing

Even when I hit the hard spots

You taught me that there would be times when

Life would appear to be all knocks.

You said to look beyond the appearances,

Seek the only truth.

Feel my Spirit within rising,

Rising as proof.

Proof of the real me,

Struggling to be born

The real me filled with laughter

And unbridled joy.

The real me facing life in a different

More powerful way.

Since I walked through our door

And, you invited me to stay.

2002

Waiting for You on a Winter's Night

Quiet snow falls lightly.
A full silver moon shines brightly.
The sky an indigo blue
My thoughts turn to you.

My mind welcomes the calm
Snow on the tree branches spread like balm
Over me.

Stars like crystal jewels
Reminds me of past Yules.
When you and I were so much in love
Nothing below or nothing above.

Matched the fire in our souls,
We set the snow ablaze on one winter's night,
Reveling in our unbridled delight.

Quiet snow and full silver moon
I wait for you to be with me again soon.

2012

When There is Love

When there is love,

The God who made it all

And, is all

Blesses the union of marriage;

Born of love.

The Universe answers with thunderous applause:

The stars display their celestial light,

Brilliance.

The lovers' reflect their love for each other,

As the moon shimmers in reflected sunlight,

Brighter.

When there is love,

The lovers glow;

The electricity of love excites the senses;

And, fills every space they touch.

Nothing in the Universe will ever be the same

As two hearts and minds unite to claim their place

In life and in love.

The magic grows with each passing year;

The celebration never ends;

When there is love.

2002

The Game

I felt his hand touch my hair

Soft and velvet.

His eyes said love

His heart wanted mine.

Soft and velvet.

We played a carefree game.

Avoiding his gentle touch.

Teasing that he displayed too much.

Teasing that he loved just me.

He laughed and told me , "Never."

Yet his heart showing through his eyes

Said, "Forever."

1979

Changes

From time to time there are changes
Some for the better
Some for the worst.

Needs of the spirit
Are not needs of the mind.

Eyes half closed
I know he sees me in the haze

Watching his game
I know that he hears me through the cheers.

Concentrating on his work
I know he is thinking of me

And, when he walks through
Through the door
I make sure that he
Touches me.

1976

To My Friend, Don Pond

Friendship is an expression of love.

It wraps lives and it weaves minds in the most

delightful and surprising ways.

With the most unlikely people.

We laughed, cried, celebrated, and grieved.

Sometimes loud and sometimes silent,

But, always friends in love.

In love with life -simple things, flowers and trinkets,

Complicated things endured and survived but shared.

Not always within reach but never out of touch.

Common minds, bonding and feeling

The etching of pathways-the trails of a

lifetime-memories.

You are that friend and forever will remain a

joyful sound in my mind.

So, this separation is not that dreaded 'good-bye'.

It is not the sorrowful farewell

But, I'll see you later, my dear and loving friend.

August 25, 2014

A Day of Not

Release felt good and bad

No seven o'clocks on Monday.

Real rest on Sunday.

Not preparation for the too early Monday risings.

Spinning deliriously in a circle

Ever tightening.

Pulling myself in from the fragments left

After the silent wars of looks, innuendos,

and miles of paper.

Pulling myself in from endless discussions

Of the same words, I knew before they were spoken.

Arising on Tuesday-declaring a day of NOT.

1997

Dream Drifter

The world sees you in control.

Your life appears orderly

You're never late.

Always on time

But you don't fool me, dream drifter.

Your star is as far away as mine.

We meet, we kiss and separately move on.

We both hear music, strange haunting songs.

We dream through life by these silent tunes.

Leading us into a future that goes pass the moon.

We will meet again as our journeys cross

Our kiss will be longer and sweeter.

But we'll leave each other as before.

Some wanderers

Like us, they seek the distant stars

They dream endless dreams of the yet unseen

And travel far.

1983

Love Found
Its Way

Crossing oceans on silken threads,

Love found its way.

Facing life's challenges without fear or dread,

Love found its way.

A mingling of spirits;

A uniting of souls;

Love had its way.

Today and forever bound as one,

The glory and joy revealed under one sun.

A single expression of Spirit.

We celebrate this day.

All because Love found its way.

2005

Relax

Like a warm blanket

The mists of your love

Surround me.

The brush of your lips on my face.

Erase the lines of the hurried times.

The presence of your body

Absorb the tensions of the stress-filled day.

The electric of your smell

The teasing of your touch

I fall

I sink

I lose myself

In you.

1985

A New Beginning

How long has it been since you bundled babies?
Rushing through traffic;
Rushing through life, it seemed nonstop
No time to realize the role model you were becoming
To admiring and watchful little eyes.

Too busy to know the values you instilled,
Too tired to care, the next day blending into the next.
Year after year, not looking back
Just looking ahead.

Little eyes growing larger,
With each year you set an example of strength
Integrity and perseverance.

Was it the love of the work?
Often you were betrayed by politics.
Was it monetary gain?
Too high a price for not enough reward.

Time has passed, too slowly then too quickly.
Children grown up;
Grandchildren with admiring eyes.

What have you really accomplished?
Is the only payoff pension and retirement?

No, you have created a benchmark for your
children and your grandchildren.
You have demonstrated the pride in self-reliance;
You have carried your burdens with dignity,
You have earned the respect of those who know you.

Today, you are honored by those who love you.
This is not retirement.
This is the beginning of reaping the harvest
that you planted so long ago.
You husband, your children, your grandchildren,
family, and friends
Celebrate your new beginning.

A new beginning based upon the foundation
that you have built.
A foundation of love, strength, integrity,
and perseverance.

1999

The Children

The children wait

Mahogany faces, honey-brown faces

Chocolate faces, vanilla faces.

Eyes of many hues

Nappy hair, straight, wavy and curls

Boys and girls.

The children wait

Some are silent

Some cry

Inside of them is hurt and confusion

They cannot question "Why?"

The children wait

For loving arms to hold them

For tender words to enfold them

For shelter from what they don't understand.

The children wait

For you.

1983

The Little Girl Played a Piano

Perched on the bench

Legs too short to reach the floor

Little hands

Stretching

For notes too far away

Bright eyes devouring

Every note on the page

Every right one

Struck

A smile

Baby face

Concentration

Grown up size determination

A little girl played a big piano today.

1976

For My Grandson

A wish fulfilled and a dream come true,

We are blessed by the presence of you.

You symbolize the hope of the future,

Beginning anew-all contained in the presence of you.

Your birth captures the very essence of life.

I marvel at your perfection and how you came to be,

Maybe that's just the grandmother in me.

But, you were born from love into love.

My belief is that the Spirit of God surrounds you

and fills you on this Blessing Day,

My prayer is that you learn as you grow on your way.

To be courageous for life will challenge your

every move,

To be brave but not foolish, life does have

often unspoken rules.

To be honest and trustworthy, a man of your word,

To be in love with life and love your life,

To be kind and compassionate, that will take you far.

To know that you have all that you need to
become who you are.
Yes, Alexander, you will not remember this sight,
Of loved ones who are gathered today, some
hoping, some praying,
All wishing you well.
My prayer is that you become the kind of man
where The Spirit will dwell.

Love always,
Grandma Charlyne

June 10, 2012

To Adrienne

My dearest granddaughter:

My prayer for you is that you continue to grow

strong in mind, body, and spirit.

My wish for you is that you will always be

guided by Truth as it is revealed to you.

My dream for you is that your dreams

will be fulfilled.

My promise to you is that I will be as much a

part of your life as you desire.

My love for you is unconditional.

Love,

Grandmama

2006

Grandmama's Wish for My Granddaughter

Dearest Granddaughter:

I loved you before you made your grand entrance
into the world. How could I not love you that
soon? My prayers of happiness for your Dad and
Mom held the hope that one day, you would be
born into our family.

You're too fresh and new to understand any of this
but when you are older, I hope that these words
find a place in your heart.

You are the promise fulfilled of new life

and new hopes and dreams.

Your life spirit embodies the life spirits of

all of your relatives, near and far.

I am filled with anticipation to watch you

grow into who you really are.

A blessing and blessed, a gift beyond compare

Your life, I want to share.

If you seek my counsel, I promise all of the

wisdom that I have at my command.

I promise you unconditional love for the

rest of my days and beyond.

Grow wise and strong, my little angel.

Know that you are loved.

June 15, 2006

Grandma's Rosary

I touched Grandma's rosary beads this morning.
They were warm as if her fingers
had just then silently glided across them in Hail
Marys and Glory Bees.
The dark black-brown beads hold a mystery.
The crucifix at the beginning. Lost somewhere
in another time. I think of replacing it but won't.
The beads are too old for something new
added. They are Grandma's rosary beads.
A gift from my dad. And, they were hers. The
only thing I have that was hers.
To hold, to let my fingers trace the path that she
wore in those warm black-brown beads.
How long did she have them? How old, I'll
never know. I imagine, yet I will know in time
when Grandma tells me.
"Chama," she called to me. "Let me plait your
hair," she sang in her broken Creole-English.
We sat on the old box in the front at night. The
silent night, warm. Warm like the rosary
beads that she kept in her apron pocket.
We shared warm French bread and a carton of

cream cheese. Not the Northern kind. The
New Orleans kind with the sugar she would
sprinkle on top.

I never heard her say the words or the silent
prayers. I knew she loved me. She kept me
close to her most of the time. To protect? There
was reason, I know that now but it didn't
help. She never knew.

Years later, I told stories to daddy about my time
with Grandma. The times that he wasn't
there to protect-the abandoned time.

He laughed at my stories of sitting on the big
box in front. He said, "Mama and me would sit
at night when everyone else was sleeping. We ate
coconut planks and drank Jumbo."

He laughed again. I could see the memories
in his eyes.

I touched the beads and could see Grandma's
beautiful brown Creole face. Smiling at me.
She smiled at me and I smiled back…a scared
little girl only smiling when I felt safe with
Grandma. One day, Grandma, we will sift the
stars together…like you did the rosary beads
and we will share secrets and eat heavenly
food…cream cheese and French bread.

Reflection

Passing a mirror

I saw my grandma's face.

My features are fading

Into her beauty and grace.

The softness and blurring

Of the eyes

I take a close look

And, hear myself sigh.

Remembering how I think of her

The sound of her voice,

Grandma made me feel safe

She gave me a shelter place.

I pause at my reflection

Of Grandma that I see

I smile knowing that she

Forever will be a part of me.

2014

Just Dad: A Tribute

It's amazing how time goes and we grow up.
You were a young man once when we were
even younger
We looked up to you as just Dad.

Your quietness was your strength
It was also our security.
We didn't know that then.
You were just Dad.

You weren't much for hugging and kissing
Or those traditional games that they say dads play.
But, we knew that you were there for us.

When you laughed our whole world knew it.
Everyone within the sound of your voice
Joined in and then the neighborhood knew it.
We were all laughing with just Dad.

As the years went by, we understood the things
that adults understand.
We began to understand the measure of a man.
As our children came and filled our lives
We could see that you were more than just Dad.

You were our first role model of love, security,
strength and honesty,
Integrity and all of the things that separate
excellence from mediocrity.
You were all that we wish to be to our children
and grandchildren and our great grandchildren.

You asked for nothing in return
You gave us all that you had to give.
We could not have asked for more
We were blessed to have you as just our Dad.

1993

Lilly: Reflections on an 88th Birthday

Loving the Lord God she serves;

Intuition that comes from years of living and learning;

Light of the Spirit that shines from within her;

Listening with a heart of understanding;

Interest in life and the joy she finds in everyday living;

Enough love that she surrounds her world in a
warm embrace.

She is known as Ma,

Mother, grandmother, great-grandmother,

aunt, and friend.

Today, how do we define her life as a mother?

It is the love that she has for all who come into

her presence?

Is it her patience in waiting for answers from the Lord?

Is it her quiet dignity and ability to offer forgiveness?

Is it the sacrifice she made for her family through

the growing years?

It is all of those things and more. We celebrate her

life because God in His Grace

Has allowed her to bless others as He continues to

bless her.

Above all, we praise and honor God and say,

"Thank-you, Father God,

For this life, this woman, your servant, and

mother to many

Known to us as "Ma"

Happy Birthday.

2009

A Young
Mother's Loss

When things happen that we do not understand
When life seems to deal just one after another
hard hand
It is not easy to see beyond the dark day
That a loving and merciful Jesus stands in our way.

We do not feel His Presence
We do not feel His Touch
We are so overcome by our grief
That we just do not know much.

There are no words of comfort
To match how we feel
Our minds are turning like the spokes on a wheel
We do not remember how to pray or to kneel.

It is too soon to embrace Him
It is too soon to rest in His Arms

But, He understands our sorrow
And will shield us from harm.

Jesus knows about sorrow
He knows about pain
He also knows that we have heaven to gain.
Yes, a loving and merciful Jesus still stands
in our way
He is ready to love and to comfort us when
we reach that day.

When we are able to fall on our knees,
with eyes on heaven,
Ready to face what we may
A loving and merciful Jesus stands in our way.

2009

Encouragement for a Friend on a Retreat

Friends become dearer to us as the months
blur into years,
We have laughed and celebrated many joys;
We have held each other up in prayer while both
shedding tears.

I have seen your faith tested,
I have seen your hope disappointed,
But through it all,
I have seen you rise up as one of God's anointed.

May God's light shine around you in all you do and say,
May you continue to set a Spirit filled example,
And, keep God's will as your chosen way.

May the peace of God find any troubled place,
That may be in your heart;
And, heal it with His mercy and grace.

May you remember to seek His precious Son

In every human face.

May this retreat bring you joy

By renewing your mind, body, and soul.

May you continue to walk in His Light

And, share God's Word

Which is more precious than gold.

2004

God Does

GOD DOES

People do not choose their true friends.

GOD DOES

He supplies each of us the friends we need in a lifetime.

I thank God for choosing you to share your

friendship and love with me.

I'm not ready for distance and time to come

between us

With its new adventures.

But, people do not choose their true friends.

GOD DOES

So, I know that you will always be there for me.

1983

On That Day In Memory

I have no words to say.

Nothing to take the hurt away.

Tears that will silently flow.

Regardless of where any of you go.

But, suffering over, peace at last,

None of the love between you

Will ever pass.

Blessed in peace, Comforted in sleep,

Waiting until that day when our

Beloved Saviour His Appointment with us to keep.

All reunited, no more tears of grief and pain.

Your loss now will one day and forever be your gain.

2011

Time for Tea (Apology to Joyce Kilmer)

I think that there should always be
A time for ladies to gather for tea.

Our most beautiful clothes we always wear
Complete with lovely hats to cover our hair.

We speak of nice things that make us laugh
We remember good things from our past.

And, the desserts that come our way
We hold our breath and begin to pray.
Oh, please don't let the calories be
Another size larger dress for me.

But as soon as we taste that first delightful bite

All care about calories quickly takes flight.

The tea warms our hearts and spirits, too

There's so much enjoyment, what's a lady to do?

So, we eat another piece of tea time cake

And, thank the hostess for the choices she did make.

We can hardly wait for Tea Time again.

We laugh out loudly and we all, "Amen."

2011

The Crowd

Alone and everyone is here
They have all assembled for the day
I arrived and will never leave
I have left and never arrived.

I watch them and listen
They speak in chaos
I listen to the noise.

Their words drift in and out
I drift in and out of their words.
Yet alone, always alone.

I see you and hear you in the room
I am blind to other faces
Deaf to other voices.
There is only you in the chaos.

Do you see me?

Do you hear me?

Am I a part of the noise to you?

Will there ever be a time for us?

A time to blot out the noise?

A time when I am not alone in the crowd

But, when I am everything to you or

Nothing at all?

Memories

What are these things called memories?

Sometimes they are flashes of a person's laughter

Other times the joy of a moment past.

Whenever they come, they are lasting bits

of a time past

They can bring a peace and comfort

For the moment when we are alone.

They fill sometimes empty hours with voices

in the room

We can see our loved ones and friends

We hear their conversations

In the replay of our minds.

These are things that time cannot tarnish

Our loved ones are ever young.

They are fresh and alive with the spirit of living.

We live to build memories and good ones are

easy to do

Sometimes we forget how easy it is to remember.

At times we tend to grieve what appears to

be lost to us

Until we remember

All that we thought we had lost is found

Within us carefully tucked away in our minds.

Carefully guarded as a treasure of the head

and the heart

Ours to share or to keep locked away for

those special moments.

Memories are the essence of life, love and all

things true.

They grow more precious with time.

And, if they are shared, they blossom and

grow into gardens of memory flowers.

Waiting for us to gather them time and

time again.

1993

Not Just Us

A single shot rings out in the night

A scream pierces the air

Who is it this time?

A black man child

Cut down like grass

So many to cry

So many to mourn

Why? Lord, was this black man child born?

Another lesson for us

Another time to grieve

When, Lord will we receive?

The American Dream

A nightmare for the Black man child

Death at the hands of a free assailant

Was he black? We do kill our own

Was he white? We have a history there we know

Was he Hispanic? A new killing field

Lord, help us to understand.

Did this black man child die for nothing?

Was he just another Coon in hunting season?

This time, Lord, it is not Just Us

The world is watching and waiting for Justice,

This time the watchers are not Just Us.

2012

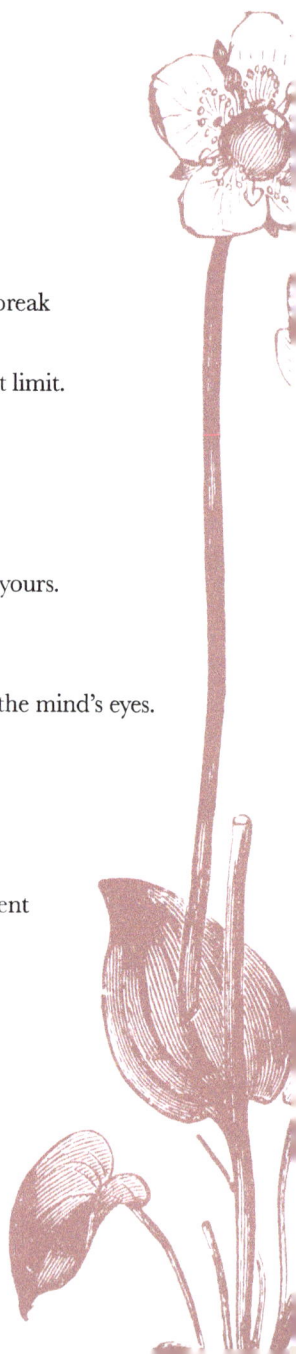

Freedom

You needed a reason, an excuse to break
Your interest spent
Your patience long tested to its short limit.
I became the cause.
The crusade to detach.
Break the bond, loose the ties.
Cut me out before I am set free.
You thought the freedom would be yours.
But, No.
I'm the one free this time.
Free from taking the pulse, reading the mind's eyes.
Feeling the tension in the room.
Magnified in me a thousand times.
Absorbing the indecision.
Applying the healing.
I grieve the loss but only for a moment
of readjustment.
As quick as your level of interest—
your depth of shallow thought.

1997

Hard-Headed Men

I know why the world is in such a mess.

Hard-headed men. That's it.

They meet in closed and poorly ventilated rooms.

Attaches click open.

They spread their papers across big tables.

Sometimes, the papers are just lists of unrelated items.

Some pull cards from inside suit pockets to jot

cryptic symbols.

Symbols that mean nothing moments after

being drawn.

In centuries to come, some archaeologists will

discover fragments and declare a rare find.

A key to why our civilization failed.

Cryptic symbols that said nothing and meant even less.

Written, scratched, scrawled by hard-headed men.

1995

The Golden Buffalo

Standing alone

With a vision

A permanent place for the

Memories of golden heroes

Though faded by time.

Existing in the minds of too few.

The vision unfolds

It has become a quest.

The flame is burning.

The birth of a monument for those

Heroes whose deeds have gone so long

Without a song

Without a resting place.

Without the praise of a nation.

They loved enough to give their

Most precious gift.

Their spirits reside in this

Steadfast symbol.

Standing alone.

Until this moment.

Can you see the flame burning?

Burning away the haze of forgetfulness.

Penetrating the fog of ignorance. The doors are

flung wide and the

Golden Buffalo no longer stands alone.

The nation has opened its heart. The vision

One step from reality. The Golden Buffalo held

fast to a vision.

And, now the time has come.

1985

Silly Little Messages

Wouldn't you rather peek
Under the bed where you sleep?
Instead of taking those secret looks
In another person's books?

Slick and sly
You've got something in your eye.
Could it be that you took a look
In someone else's book?
Don't try to hide
We know you are the spy.

Slave - My Land, My Country

Over the land

Over the sea

My country calls to me.

Ripped from its shores

Torn from its soil

Brought to this new world

A slave to toil.

Betrayed by my brothers

Stolen from our mothers

Sweat on my brow

Pulling and pushing a plow.

Longing to go back

I just don't know how.

This new country speaks to me

My country 'tis of thee' I sing

Land of the Pilgrim's pride.

Land where I slave and die.

1997

The Legacy

The history books tell stories
About our time as slaves.
There are thousands upon thousands
Of our unmarked graves.
Faces we have never seen.
Ancestors we don't know.
Just stories about our slave days
So long ago.
But, there are wonderful stories
That sing of our glory days.
Stories of a strong people
Who were giants in many ways.
Slavery could not put out our fire.
It raised our expectations and our desires.
Slavery forged unbreakable bonds
Slavery made us more fearless and brave.
Our ancestors still shout encouragement from
their unmarked graves.

We are a part of those proud people.

Walking boldly into the night.

And, everywhere we step.

We can leave a patch of light.

1990

The Spirit of God is Moving

The Spirit of God is moving

Across the face of the day

'The Spirit of God is moving

In radiance

A blaze of orange brilliance

Breaks the rosy glow

Climbing from the East

The Spirit of God is moving

Clouds to reveal the true nature of day

In warmth and light

Spirit Light

Lifts my soul as the Spirit of God is moving

Kissing my face as the sky also receives

The Spirit's Presence

I close my eyes

Facing the Light

I see colors

Vibrant, healing

Energy surging through my being

Into my soul

Wake Up!

Arise from your sleep.

The colors say

The Spirit of God is moving.

1996

Women, You Hold the Power

They have numbed you into an existence.

This is the only freedom they allow you.

But, then they condemn you for taking that only

choice. Just enough cards to get your

Rationed food for your mouths to feed.

Scorned, yet needed by the many to provide a

reason for those high paid salaries.

Where will they be without you and your

hungry mouths?

You fill their pockets

You fill their jails

You give them daily news

News from the Hell that you struggle to escape.

They promise to help

You die every day in poverty and neglect

In your innocence, you believe them once again.

You lose your hopes and dreams.

Will you awaken to the truth?

You hold the power.

Look up! You have nothing to be ashamed.

Face your accusers.

Change your focus. Feel your power.

They are nothing without you. You provide for them.

Stop! Use your voice. Say, "No" and watch

them squirm.

See your richness. Claim your power.

The world waits for You.

1997

To See The Spirit

When you look in the mirror,

Do you see the Spirit of God?

When you open your mouth to speak,

Do you hear the Word of God?

The Spirit within shows on your face;

Living for Christ,

We magnify God's Grace.

2005

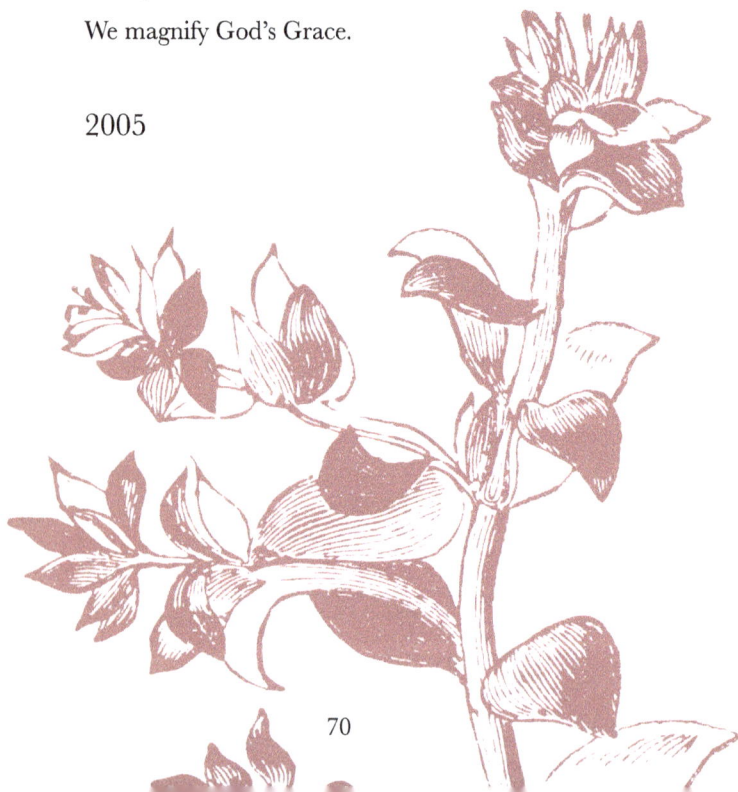

Request

While on your journey stop if you will

Think about me if you happen to see a stream

Perhaps, flowing pass a hill and near it a tree

Gentle and still.

The tree is like me

Planted with roots, unable to roam.

Yet, still free.

The hill is like me

Rising a little above the ground.

Yet, very much earthbound.

The stream is like me

Gentle at times and controlled by the air.

Enjoying the storm.

Yet, enjoying weather fair.

It is a lot to ask, but please do it for me.

And, be ever so grateful to be, totally free.

1983

Uncommonly Death

Why is that as common as death is, we never
realize how it still shocks and jolts.
Brutal no matter how peaceful
Brutal no matter how anticipated
Brutal in its assault on life.

We watch in anguish
We writhe in its finality
No reprieve
Even for the faithful as well as the faithless.

Death smashes dreams yet unrealized
Robbing and stealing masquerading as natural
It is not.

It is a ghastly and horrible joke
Cruel in its assault on the suspecting and
the unsuspecting

Yet in its wake, we awaken to its reality
For the faithful in a hope in a resurrection
For the faithless
I don't know.

I just know the pain and the suffering
The vacant house
The unanswered phone
Erasing the number
Erasing all evidence of who lived there.

The nightmare of it finally over
The memories of alive today
Death claiming its prize tomorrow.

I do have faith in the resurrection
But for right now
Awakening to a deep silence and sadness
That is loud and profound and not
understanding
But accepting because there is no choice.

Hope is the answer
Faith the foundation of that anticipation
That there is a reuniting
A reconciliation
An eternity.

2014

Shadow in Your Life

I am a shadow in your life

Always on the fringes,

Never far away

Never close enough to touch you.

We are separated by darkness

In the light, I exist with you

But, only as a shadow in your life.

You see me in sunlit hallways,

You see me in softly lighted rooms

You have reached out your arms to me

Only to be startled by the presence of darkness.

Then you seek the dark that separates me from you.

You seek darkness because you are afraid.

Afraid of yourself and what you may find by

embracing a shadow.

The power of your world demands that you

Choose the darkness.

The darkness that will keep me separated from you.

We only exist in sunlit hallways

And, in softly lighted rooms.

I will remain a shadow in your life.

Always on the fringes,

Never far away,

Never close enough to touch you.

1983

Spring

Fragrant newness
Silky blossoms
Winter's promised flower
Kissed by a gently shower.

1986

Summer's Night

Moon bright

Magic light

Lilac smells

Bird songs swell

Moon bright

Magic night

Voices sweet

Lovers meet

Moon bright

Summer's night.

1985

Rites of Spring

Spring brings birth through Nature in spite of a
sometimes wintry scene or two.

We are a part of Nature's pattern, just look at
me and you.

We chose this day in April to seal a pledge.

To love each other true.

That's not so different from the birds and budding trees,

And, the spring flowers that embrace the dew.

We bring our gifts of loyalty, passion, and quiet romance,

We invite our hearts to share in Nature's dance.

This is our birth, a new life.

It trembles with the anticipation of great promise.

We shape it with a foundation of love,

We behold its beauty in this quiet moment of eternity.

As the willow tree sways and bends to the wildest wind.

Our pledge of love will weather the storm.

We will seek shelter in each other's love.

1994

Nature's Play

Sitting on a river bank in a secret place
Small lazy ripples licking our feet like the tongues
Of many puppies.

A soft gentle breeze, kissing our sun-caressed bodies
We are both golden in the sun.
Nature loves us both the same.

Bank grasses sway a ballet
As birds carry the tune.

Time passes and the sun-down actors
Prepare their praise song to the moon.

Sitting on a river bank in a secret place,
Moonlight greets us in a coating of shimmering
silver-white.
Nature loves us both the same.

Crickets strike up their tune
The willow tree begins her love dance
As the breeze plays through her hair like fingers
Love-touch a harp.

You gather me close
We sit close and still.
There are no words for us to say.

We are a part of Nature,
Waiting,
For our parts in this, Nature's play.

1976

www.ingramcontent.com/pod-product-compliance
Lightning Source LLC
Chambersburg PA
CBHW050819090426
42737CB00021B/3449